MOON: LETTERS, MAPS, POEMS

MOON: LETTERS, MAPS, POEMS

JENNIFER S. CHENG

TARPAULIN SKY PRESS
CA ∴ CO ∴ NY ∴ VT
2018

Moon: Letters, Maps, Poems
© 2018 Jennifer S. Cheng
ISBN-13: 9781939460158
Printed and bound in the USA

Cover art by Maude Tanswai.

Tarpaulin Sky Press
P.O. Box 189
Grafton, Vermont 05146
www.tarpaulinsky.com

For more information on Tarpaulin Sky Press trade paperback and hand-bound editions, as well as information regarding distribution, personal orders, and catalogue requests, please visit our website at tarpaulinsky.com.

For my Loved One, G.

And for all the mythical women of my childhood:
Chang 'E, Nü Wa, the Snake Sisters, and Goddess Tin Hau.
In these stories: a lady in the moon, a creator in a world flooded over,
a reptile becoming woman and back again, a guardian of the seas.

Table of Contents

{ And if this house was in ruins? And if these ruins were the desert? It is the broken stone, it is every grain of sand that would then answer for our passage. }

- E. Jabès, trans. P. Joris

.

{ Beneath it is all dark, it is all spreading, it is unfathomably deep; but now and again we rise to the surface and that is what you see us by. }

- V. Woolf

.

{ Bewilderment as a poetics and an ethics. }

- F. Howe

{ PRELUDE } : SEQUESTERINGS

i.

In the story of the Lady in the Moon, she begins on earth. In the story of the Lady in the Moon, there is a pill, an elixir, that keeps her breath from stopping. There is, depending on the story, her motive to spare the world of a man who should not live forever, or there is her naiveté, her childish impatience, or sometimes an accident. She flees or she is floating. In the story of the Lady in the Moon, there is only one ending: to live out her nights as a captive, over and over, as if some necessary penance, as if a sorrow to see a woman paper-thin against the lesser light.

ii.

*Sometimes it helps to say it through a seashell. The sound of it
washed in waves, loud yet silent, trailing in and out. Sometimes it
wants to be said with a slowness that looms, an hour giving way to
cloud and fog, the way it starts outside my window, twenty blocks
to the shore, and drifts gradually toward me until my apartment,
four floors up, is immersed in a pale envelope.*

*

If I could say, here is a woman watching her house come undone.

Or: Sometimes in order to build something, you must unbuild it first.

*

*A myth is a narrative we are given as children. It comes to us whole
and all surface. It says: A Lady is trapped on the moon because
she is a bystander. It says: A Lady had no intentions of leaving the
ground and floating toward the sky. It says: She has no home, her
body is not hers to wield.*

*

*When we set about infusing a voice, where do we begin? Its
shadow spaces, half-obscured corners, the ellipses at the tail of its
third breath. The sound that cowers is usually the one that rings
deepest. Is most true. To find the center, I turned toward the edges
fraying in the dark. Perhaps I was looking for its broken parts.
Perhaps I wanted to un-know a myth. We intuited the holes, we
knew they were there, we only meant to locate them.*

*

The parts of her voice that are cloudy, like a dark tea as it is beginning to steep. Her voice in the moment of expanding or contracting. Before or after or in the vapor, which is to say, not the actual events themselves but their condensations. The damp pause between inhalation and exhalation. When nothing is happening but everything. The in-between that no one tells.

*

If a woman's voice is a space that begins boundaried in. If there was something I wanted to speak into the air, the clotted atmosphere, if I thought to myself, the edge of her dress, my fingers in her hair. *If it was ruin, and I carried it heavy and spilling in my belly, a breadth too immense for my own. So I wanted to say it to the corner of the room. So I borrowed the shape of her mouth.*

*

What texture, what temperature, what manner of weather? Something with which to spread our body so it is no longer buried. We are ever finding ourselves too large for the clothes on our backs, their knitted borders yet herding us in, a protective outer layer. If I meant to shutter anything, it was only so I could see how thick and deep the midnight tidewater goes.

*

(If a closure of lines is always a lie. If shadows are multiple because the body is multiple. If, then, a continuation, the moon in its phases. Bewilderment and shelter, destruction and construction, unthreading as it rethreads, shedding as it collects.)

*

I wanted to say: a new aesthetics of domesticity. I wanted to say: she.

7

*

If she *is.*

If she *holds.*

*

There is upheaval in small spaces. A world comes untethered in a pinprick. In a crack in the door jamb, in a dust pile under the bed. When the rain comes, sometimes I find I have always been waiting with my ear to the ground.

*

Her voice is the rhythm of sleepwalking. In sleep we are no better than animals. In sleep the moon is a magnet that regulates our breath. A body that sleepwalks abandons as much as it accumulates: pathways, murmurings, attempts of the appendages. It happens when the body is suspended in quiet chaos: night, sleep. Let us haunt the air with a small uneven-tempered earthquake. We are always reporting on the stirrings surrounding our bodies.

*

To dress in the intimacy of second-hand clothing: to wear something, like a sweater, that has been stretched by the warmth of another's frame: to know that each loose patch, each gathered seam, holds the ghostly imprint of another's movements: a bodily knowledge: a layering of echoes: to take an object historically defined and set its borders in motion.

*

Things disintegrating even as they take on mass. We are, if anything, in tension.

{ I } : ITERATIONS

1.

Perhaps it begins with the day before she left, not forever but for a lifespan, so that when she touched him on the arm, they began to cry. If it were honest, perhaps it would begin with everything in the margins: how they married young, how she stopped leaving the house, how between two blinking lights she saw a dark spot grow.

2.

The lady in the moon loved her husband, but one day she left him on the earth in order to fly into the midnight, the edges of her dress like a decaying moth's arms. She wanted to live on the light of the moon. Or: The lady in the moon was banished from the heavens along with her husband. Alone with her sadness, she found the capsule under a piece of red silk and swallowed it, forgetting to save half for the man she loved. Or: The lady in the moon wanted to save the world from the reign of the man she had married, and so she stole the elixir of eternal life.

3.

The lady in the moon loved her husband, who was the kind of man who could shoot down nine suns with a bow and arrow in order to save the world. Then, to save his wife, he gave her a pill from beyond the ends of the earth, but gave it to her twice, as if he did not need his own. Filled with the secrets of another world, her body began rising to the moon like a balloon let loose or smoke from a graven fire. And here his heart lies in pieces, broken pottery shards on the dusty floor. When she was gone, vanished into the stonecracked sky, he built for himself a dwelling on the sun made of mulberry branches and gold, so that he might be nearer, so that there in the sky he might meet his wife once a year on the fifteenth day of the eighth moon, when the moon is brightest and filled with water.

4.

The lady in the moon loved her husband, but one night she came home covered in chalky dust that turned under the light, and then he knew. He knew the sickly smell of moon branches on her skin, he knew where her body had been. The taste of water in her mouth was filled through with the uttermost parts of the night.

5.

(And when they neared, so orbitally slow, he could feel the bone coldness emanating from her body, like phosphorescent fingertips reaching forward.)

6.

He can smell the wet bark of the mangrove tree in her hair, the vines and fresh dirt of rain newly fallen in a world at the edge of things. He can smell the earthen cloves mixed with dampened leaves and thickly knotted roots. The foreign air from a ripened land that hangs precipitously in the dark. And he knows that she, too, can sense the dust of nine dead sun children, bitter-smelling and rotten, on the skin of his fingers and the quiver of his bow.

7.

The lady in the moon wanted to listen to cicadas humming against the evening tide; she wanted to watch insects disappear into sunken parts. She said to herself, *there are finer days than these.*

8.

In the story of a woman who angles her face outward instead of down, the moon is an island where trees grow from rock, and stones layer like waves. In the story of a woman who dreams at night of varying wildernesses and a different kind of emptiness— *where might your weather be?* she asks. She asks, for once, for more.

9.

For after the earth began shaking and tree leaves sprinkled with dirt began to fall in a crinkly, untidy mess, and after cracks began to deepen, after shadows turned a violent shade of bone, the lady in the moon felt her gaze shift. And when she touched the red silk, the strangely lit square of fabric, stranger than anything she had touched before, she felt a wrinkle in her heartbeat. Her heart began to wrinkle, and she placed her hand on it, as if to say, *here.* Suddenly there were ladders to the heavens, giant wheels in the underworld, oceans to sail in the hollow of an emptied-out fruit. Suddenly the sky was a canopy.

10.

The lady in the moon woke at the hour before every evening to watch the sun set and the moon rise above a dirty lake. The phoenix thought she had come to see him and his fiery plumes, but it was the moon she loved, the moon she woke for. She sat with her legs dangling over rocks and algae and abandoned boats. For the lady in the moon had been a child full of fears, a body in constant hesitation. If she could, she would fill a wet bucket of gritty mollusks and meander beyond such marshes. And perhaps one day the lady in the moon will fall for the angles of the forest. Or perhaps, one day it will be this same forest where she saves a wild rabbit's life. Slowly, but surely, she will find her way to the sky.

11.

The moon pulled on her body as it pulled on the waters of the earth.

12.

And what does one give up, in order to be a hero? What lives are eroded from the sky in a murmuring blaze? He had said he was tired of looking after things; she could see it in his posture. For here we have the lady in the moon as a child of the earth: first a child of her parents, then a child of her husband. For although the archer and his wife were banished together to the parched fields, on earth he was given to be a hero. He knew how to keep the animals penned, he knew how to bring the food home. The tree branch stuck in the middle of the tide could never belong to her because he was always there beside her, the shadow of his arm was always obstructing it. He grew larger as she crept smaller, yet still she could see how his bow grew heavy, how it began to splinter under her weight.

13.

The lady in the moon did not take with her: rubber boots, the view of the sea, her glass jars. She took with her relics of childhood, an imaginary map (*X marks the spot*), and two fingernail moons. And when she arrived, smeared in the incandescent ash of thousand-year-old dead, she built a house through which aberrant light traveled from one window to the other, and there she sat, and there she left her home every afternoon, and there the child stars reeled in drunken delight.

14.

For the lady in the moon stole an ethereal herb and escaped her husband. She is the faithful wife, the jealous lover, the embittered woman of sorrow; but she is never the hero. No, the hero requires a skill beyond hers, a grounded knowledge of cosmological directions, a bagful of sharpened gold blades, and the lady in the moon has only her desire, her unmentioned lack of regret. She floats unrooted, full of longing for the arctic sky, opening farther and farther; and it is her husband who seeks to be near, who rides the sun, who measures the revolutions of the moon, maps out the intersections of orbits.

15.

No longer to ask for safe passage, for someone to return. No longer to board herself up to make the world smaller. If the lady in the moon held a seascape in her belly. No longer to hide the things that make her weak; let us let them see the morning, they may grow in new directions.

16.

A deviation of celestial bodies: a variation. For there was no warning, no rearing, no years of implicit preparation. No one taught her to feel a gap in place of a space of her own. She swam across the midnight sea and alighted with a handful of shiny rocks. White quartz, black siltstone, fossilized ammonite. The loneliness of an emigrant is the soaking of light just before sunset.

17.

And when he reaches over and stretches out his fingers, ignoring the shiver that crawls up his arm, the lady in the moon is already distracted by the mass of half-translucent clouds resting on the mountain outside her window, its color a shade of diluted tea, glazed pottery, tepid bone gray resting in the pulp of a winter lake.

18.

For inside their earthly house, she'd mourned the empty jars, cried over the pile of buttons, grew melancholy from the unopened can of pickled lettuce. Inside the house, an old absence brewed until she could not cross a threshold. The lady in the moon: a stranger in the country surrounding her. A visit to a once-childhood-home, her husband would prescribe when he returned to find her crowding the bathroom floor. He had not known that in the empty shell of evening, the insects would trill, *Peng Chau, Cheung Chau, Tung Lung Chau...* He had not known that instead of a visit, she would float like a papery insect, and then float on.

19.

How to unsettle a compass? she asks, once more. Then she might know how to merge with the squid-ink sky and follow her body home. In dreams, the body slips in and out of secret places. To be captivated rather than captured. If the lady in the moon finds a banyan tree under which to rest, she will meet a hare and use his stone mortar and pestle to grind the pill into a fine starchy powder with which to cover the earth, preparing it for sleep.

20.

And isn't it a good thing, to be alone, to stand on one's own feet? To wake every morning and return every evening after the luminary hills have darkened and can barely be made out and, turning one's face toward the slopes, say to oneself, *this is where I live?*

21.

The lady in the moon planted a garden of tiny bulbous trees, stout and muscular.

22.

(Her chalky fingers. The smell of death on his hands. She dreams at night of the dead children lying on a river plain of shallow muddy water, the glare of their bones turning to stricken dust.)

23.

The pill was never hers, it was never something belonging to her alone. She obtained it secretly, or guiltily, or full of chastity and possibly penance, but its beginning was always with someone else. Sitting mysteriously in the corner of a room, tucked into the dark folds of her mouth as she lay dead to the world, could the moon really grow a garden, the house really veined with plumbing, with such an ominous inception? Her body will lie among silt and sediment and roots and stems. If she remembers her children yet unborn, she will think of them bathed on a salt flat and of gifts to give them that fit underneath a piece of paltry fabric: briny plum, translucent jade rabbit, crusted oyster shell. She will touch the mud-pressed scars like dried up estuaries hidden underneath her clothes and wonder how the light changes as the earth rolls forward in the corner of her window. *She is the Moon, she is the Water, she is Cold, she is Autumn and Winter, she is the Shadows.* The things that bind a woman. Or anchor her to home.

24.

A woman is a builder; she builds two homes. One is an organ, the other she takes. If the lady in the moon were to ask questions of construction, if she were to ask for tools and then drown the blueprint, bleaching blue ink till it divulged blue tears. If she spent days with her feet steeped against a rock, cheek creased in the shallow drift. If she gathered weeds, bramble, and clay to mix with the pill's ashes. If she wanted not to lose *herself* but to *lose herself*—

25.

And the moon will come to her in dreams made of water, on shadowy afternoons, wrapped up in peculiar childhood memories. The moon is made of salt, quarried rock, the moisture of the monsoon season, blurry rainwater, an ever-changing coastline. Her husband will know her by the dirt under her fingernails, a telling sign. And the *smell of the darkly cratered harbor*, she will think to herself, knowing that gravity, magnetism, and the science of the universe cannot explain the unfastening of her bones.

26.

The lady flew to the moon, and her heart grew gnarled and brittle, like the winter bones of a bonsai tree. If it turns into stone, she will have nothing to give to her future children. In some versions, she becomes a toad. In others, she is a moon goddess. What is the weather in between two points, she asks, before the pill begins to wear off? What is the difference between a crescent and a fingernail if they are both singed pollen inside a handful held close to the ground?

27.

One day the lady in the moon grew to love another: home, land. She took two planks of lumber and nailed them together. Or: she took two steps toward the watery boundary and felt its teeth lap her knees. Or: she touched two fingers to the front of her ribcage and sensed two sounds pressing back. *To be known and to be alone.* For home and for wilderness. To belong and to long.

28.

Let us say there were not any dead children, not the cruelty of a husband gone wrong. There would still be a world on the brink of bereavement. A body waning at the edge of someone else's precision. The sky is a canopy so that one may slide up against it and understand that to feel lost is a frightening feeling, and yet *caught* and *lost* can also mean the same thing.

29.

For she was never the one intended to leave. It was her husband who was called to save the world from scorched lands and fiery fields, her husband who was given the pill. After a while there was nothing left to mourn. And how was she to know the mangrove trees would be so damp, the rain so fragrant, the forests sunk in the grit and ghost of another world? The exiled light stewed inside her skin. For if it is not the man and his sinewy bow, if it is not the youthful sun gods, not the rabbit, then what it is, for the lady in the moon, is the smell of the blackened soil marred through her fingers and the papery leaves rough with salt. It is the bed against the glass, the sheets newly laundered, the knot of wrinkled chili hanging in the windowlight. It is the long walk home every night in darkness. For at night when she is exhaling into the last soot of air, tinged with the hint of a thousand feral glaciers, and knows she is alone, it is the very fact of her lonely body traveling for days through bright celestial bodies, which were like moldy fish puncturing the sky.

30.

The night was not clear, the weather full of shadows, and she became lost among debris. She found herself on a cold bright rock suspended in the middle of a dark ocean. This is how it began: with a towering tree over ten thousand feet high, with an umbrella of leaves feeding hungry infant silkworms, with deafening loneliness and a speck in her throat, with a mortal body, weighted and heavy, with quiet justification, a spell under breath, *it is never enough potency between such bodies.*

31.

The lady in the moon: the archer, the arrows, the naughty children of greater light, the three-legged crows of another world, god of the eastern sky, queen mother of the west, mythical mulberry, twelve moon children, the peach, the pill, the elixir of life, the rabbit, the forest, the woodcutter, the eternal mortar and pestle.

32.

It is no longer her fear of what is unknown. She had meant to return, will one day return, but by then the pill itself had changed, inside her body it had become something else; years of pounding and grinding would not make it fine enough. A woman who desires too much in this world is a woman who is cursed, and the woman who is cursed inevitably finds one hand empty.

33.

A woman is a lady is a goddess is a virgin is a child. Or she is a shadow, a temptress, a hindrance, a fool. *Instead*: An unsettling distance, unmoored. She flew to the light of the moon.

{ II } : ARTIFACTS

What She Left Behind

a lampshade embroidered with blue string; a fan stretched like
skin, gone brittle and slit; one jar with a lightbulb taped to its
lid; three twigs tied together and strapped to a box; a broken
hem; a bagful of salt; mornings of fog and late hours amassing
in a pile of stillness; their bed frame; their bed sheets; the shelf
he hung for her, a cabinet crowded with bowls, cups, jars, vases,
empty vessels, amputations—

Places She Will Roam

little island in the South China Seas : the return of once
homeward light : celestial equator : wandering stars (planets
that deviate from their path) : constellations that cannot sleep
below the horizon : *moon that grows smaller as it grows closer to
the sun—*

Things She Will Make

instead of a shelf of books next to the window: corners and
angles. instead of a pot of soup or saucer of congee: steam,
vapor. instead of night: how it begins: small.

her insect script, letters she sent, pieces and folds she kept,
tucked in her distances, uneven lines.

an array of seashell parts: marooned constellation. waiting for
the tide to wash them out to the center of the horizon. what
does it mean to forego the shoreline, one way or the other—

What She Left Behind

symmetry of mornings; the body in bed, and the body layering;
a cloud

could break it; a climate; a kitchen; a pillow; a doorknob; a
spine; a limb; an inch of turbulence;

eventually, the roof, the walls, the framework, sounds outside
flattened between vertical distance and lumber and glass;
eventually, jars of seeds re-homed from their woods, afraid
of the world too large, we are constantly excising to make it
smaller, eventually the walls the blinds the curtains a space so
small to move to inhale the body catatonic, eventually the house
a hole the sun and she was only ever watching it closed;

mornings like loose gravel, a thousand threads, decaying

hull; someone else's house—

Maps

a confluence of planes. between the hours. there and there and here and there—

Her Dreams At Night

they had to do with navigation. how to locate her way through
the world. how to be a part of the crescented forest without
being

lost, a framing of the body.

once she was crawling through a tunnel made of fabric unable to
see the sky. to find a tear in the cloth, an eyelet of

fear, which is to say, *what is the body in transit? a pilgrimage*—

Her Voice

because *weaving, knitting, knotting*. because *a chorus, fugue, the song cycle*. because she said, *a cone of salt, a way of moving around it*. because *becoming*. because some things are formed only through rupture: sea waves, the after-life of skies, a wholeness of continent. because the *plot of light, water, house, self, space*.

because a story, a narrative: *a place where we get to forget something, as much as remember*. because more than where we are going, our bodies displacing air, again and again. because, she thinks, an ethical matter: the logic of dust, cloud, *spiral—*

Her Voice

textures

measurements, expanding
and contracting, like fallen
sails: the hour receding

nightfall: geometry of waves, creases

bright spores transpiring on gray rock

gathering   by hand—

Her Voice

they began with the word *sequesterings*—

{ III } : BIOGRAPHY OF WOMEN
IN THE SEA

Nü Wa

If, for instance, you take the story of the girl who was saved in a hollowed gourd the size of a small boat while the rest of the world was a watery grave; if you take the story of how she floated for days, peeking over the tepid rind of the melon onto the tops of houses, street stalls, bodies of children submerged underwater, pale and bloated and gray; how at the bottom of the muted soup were paper factories and wooden spoons, jars of pickled radish, and toenails; how she saw the particles of crumbled buildings floating like dirty mist or soiled light, how she imagined dipping her hand and cupping it around the sand of those dirty particles together in her palm till they were something to hold, clumped and cold; if you take how she journeyed in utter silence, sailing in no particular direction across an endless and unbounded sea, dull lukewarm water melting into overcast sky, waiting for the waters to recede, waiting to land, somewhere, anywhere—you will remember, above all else, how she is—motherless, childless, godless—the last girl on earth—how the story of the world begins with her, a body in the marshes, sleeping, alone.

Snake Sisters

And we know that when she woke, alone in her wooden bed, the second sister was aware that the earth and the heavens were somehow misaligned. We know it was something in the air—in the smell of wood laden with moisture, or in the smoke of mountains carried in from outside. A strange, musty odor, perhaps, or a dullness where it was once crisp. We know that she woke and rushed into her sister's bedroom, where she saw a body that was missing and a body that was now slender, serpentine. Water coiled at her feet. But it was not the missing body that troubled her, not the lack of imprint or shadow, not the hole where something—anything—should have been. It was, instead, the fluidity of bones, flesh, tissue that caused her to tremble, it was the sudden

transformation of a body in the night. The utter change that overtakes a body against secluded light, without warning or attention or expectation of any sort. It was the body suddenly made strange to oneself. For the very day that the two sisters descended from their child-home to live in this nest of smoky green hills and boat-covered waters, amongst these villagers and their residences intercepted with wild banyan roots, she was not thinking of her body. She was not thinking of how its skin might grow luminous in the salt of unfamiliar moons, how sleep might be erratic and constantly interrupted; she was not thinking of how the body might grow to cradle the shadow of a cavernous mountain.

Chang 'E

And here past the hills, we have the shape of a woman flying away from the earth; she left her husband under a bird's eye view.

And here we have the moon, bending its shadow toward the earth, and then away again.

Chang 'E

For as long as the stars do not seem to align in an orderly manner, as long as such lost light sources make their way into the spinning crevices of her lungs, she will continue to ask herself: *How does one make a habitation of it? What is the relationship between a woman's fragments and her desire*

for wholeness? What does a body know better when it is alone. It radiates in multiple directions

and cannot be caught in a fistful. She collects postcards of abandoned churches, illegal housing structures, storm-hued temples. She takes photographs of burning coils dangling from the ceiling and pays homage to the oldest tree in the village, on which wishes hang in pink string and plastic oranges. We lay down roots, and then we find the terrain has cracks, like skytop branches of a dark Manzanita. For in a world where boundaries are slowly slipping, we begin with a map of the body in motion.

Nü Wa

But what is the body inclining toward—what has it already betrayed? The girl who floats for days atop a watery world does so knowing that beneath this reflective-pool reality is a world that has already been lost. It is a dull, breaking sound in her chest that she chooses to ignore like the other side of a damp mountain. Once, before the waves had come, she traveled to a tiny nearby island and for a week sat like a mollusk on a wooden plank and watched the inhabitants and the water preening the shoreline, feeling for the first time what it would be like to fever away into morsels of land decomposing off the coast, to escape far away, to settle down in an unknown place and make such emptiness

your own. What is she willing to give up for this milky expanse, for the branch of a darkened tree that appears, twisted and mirthful against a flattened seascape? She can hardly keep her breath, she thinks, and somewhere simmering in this over-saturated earth is a path of piled red rocks cast like a dam, a place where someone ought to build a home.

Goddess Tin Hau

For we know: the corpse of a sibling, her brother, somewhere at the bottom of the ocean, the moorings—

She swims through the thick waters, day until night, moon unto sun, sounding for the deflection of a warm earth-marked body. Fish belly graze underneath her legs, murky creatures intertwine her hair. Long fingerlings of seaweed, and sudden underpasses of escarpment. Her eyes fill with seawater. There is no search for other worlds except for that of warm bodies. First of father and brother. Then, of one's own.

After it is all over, the villagers will ask her, *Was it cold? Did it capture your body, prickle your skin?*

Snake Sisters

Inside her dress, an envelope. Inside her dress, disembodied [   ].
Stitching of her girlish traces, maw-soaked daydreams—we
could call it shadow-play, a bowl of wishbones, fish skeletons, or
everything you need

to unwind those lines. Inside her dress: embodied prescriptions.
I was trying to say *somewhere here* while also *nothing to fear*. I was
holding a stick, tracing circulars in the dirt. *To tell you a compass,*
to say you our organs and their weathervane hours. Or:

a nest is a hiding place for animals of the earth that slip away and
defy the ground. And what is the boundary of a girl anyway?
Misremember her childhood: a pocket with which to catch
satellite light, a collar with which to betray misplaced flesh, a
hem to invert inside.

Chang 'E

Because her husband in the fields, working the grain into sturdy patterns his body never fractured. Because she in her lull watching for the murmuring orbit of a faraway home, or a slighter confusion of the earth. Because he will make her a house at the top of a hill, and

at the bottom of the garden, under the overhang of acacia trees, she will build herself a disheveled shed in which to house all the tiny pieces: an oak nut as if a little heart, two pinecones a small lung. To build a house: one is for shelter, the other to unfold, and in the distance is the difference between sunlight in a field and the lesser seen light of the other sky.

Chang 'E

Sun-earth-moon space. Either the body nearest to the celestial surface, or the signal it sent. Either something *tiny*

in open space, or an astronomical observation. If in the *thickness of lunar soil*, it discovers the world at its depths, then "between the earth

and the moon"; then neither invisible nor covered in reflected light; then a topographical

map *shrouded in mystery.*

Nü Wa

Or: Ground, a continuous plane and persistent reference point. Whose plane, whose point, whose two feet.

She wove a cartogram made of sticks to overlay: the pattern of swells, the meanderings of waves.

What appears to be terra firma was likely water not so long ago.

Goddess Tin Hau

After that, there was no turning back. After that, I took a walk to the edge of town to clear my mind and pretend that the vegetation repelling from the coast were blooming islands, born from below. I blamed it on the angle of the day, the light askew, the wind rife with holes. *A heart is a hollow muscle, an organ ready to deflate.* When I was a child, they said *silent girl*. As if sounds could not cascade in the dark. One day they would call me: *thousand-mile eye*. I watched the mangroves spread like a blanket across our waters, branches and leaves weaving a sky for drowsy mussels, weary clams, and overwintering prawns. I saw the silhouette of my shadow as it crept along the shaky bridges between our rows of boxy stilt houses: scrap wood, sheet metal, tall wooden pegs

thrush in the underlying earth. When I was a child I never swam. I never went in past the knees. Surrounded by saline, my mother taught me to dry a cuttlefish, pickle a plum, brown a quail's egg inside a jar, but never how to pucker my fingers and toes. I turned the shell of a crab into billowy yellow skin, and I held it to the sun. My mother strapped the hull of a gourd to my back, and I felt myself buoyed. Once, while lying in the sun like a flattened mackerel, I sunk into a deep dream: an accompaniment of blood like ribbons in slow-motion air. I reached out to touch them, and my mother shook me awake.

Chang 'E

And when she feels for someone deeply, she touches them lightly on the arm while averting her eyes toward the opposite direction, into an empty space. It is either the intimacy she is trying to temper, or it is a simultaneous desire to be

unmoored. For years she slept curled in the shadow of someone else's curvature, where she was uncontested and safe. She awoke every morning to a blank day, and yet her mind was perpetually veiled, overcast in heavy-set cloth. She lay in her bed as if it were a boat in the middle of absolute stillness, she grew afraid of beating wings and small noises. In those years she read about people who hid themselves in shut-in rooms, and as she read, she thought of the brittle edges of shadow puppets lying in an old trunk, unseen yet fluttering in paper-thin musings.

Chang 'E

To say that the act of a woman is the act of a foreigner, an immigrant, to set itself to and from these coordinates.

For a body in travel is above all loosening itself, the slow migration of tectonic plates. It is the contradiction of losing homeland in search of homeland, it is the rules it breaks, the displacement it shapes, the silence of a hem torn and hemmed with thread, made up after all by some perforation of gravity—

For *distant planets and other objects;* for *meteorology;* for *mapmaking.*

Look: moon as the motion that is undoing in this moment.

Snake Sisters

It was the liturgy, perhaps, of a bodily encroachment in a world
we are always attempting to make sense of. If *she* is taught to be
scared of *her* own shadow impressing into and disclosing

the earth: whose shape, whose movements, whose hunger—

Goddess Tin Hau

Then one day—what? Her foot falling forward as if to catch herself, and she saw it could be like this all the way to the peak. At the top, it was all mist, water dripped from her eyelashes and she could not help but be moved. To move oneself, to move beyond, to lose sight of, an exhale. The sky tepid and open-mouthed. *One holds a large cloud in the throat at all times.* Later, she thought it was the confluence of fear and desire one feels when approaching a cliffside after ascending something steep or beholding the sea on an overcast morning: rickety stems of the house, all things can break, pour over. *To never know what the body might plot when it sits on the floor with piles of grieving salt—*

At night the villagers set lanterns out to drift. We go searching for what we have lost, and what returns? Something seeps like an understanding of exile, it is a dark mold spreading in the lungs. Her father had once harbored the warning signs: how she made unforgiving structures in the rooms, an even smaller cot in the bed; how speech was something that thinned and became estranged outside the home; how she tiptoed through shadows on the ground as if they were shallow ends of a shore. Now she walks to the edge of her water town, thinking of lightboxes and telescopes. When she finally sleeps, she dreams that small animals are eating at her limbs

as she tries to keep from drowning. The pain is not an acute one of sorts; surprisingly, it feels like numbing.

Snake Sisters

Suddenly the second sister remembers: long ago, they spent a night sleeping in a narrow boat with a thatched hut. All night she could feel the water moving underneath her. There are two kinds of aloneness, she realizes, the first is what you already know at the top of a mountain, looking downward through the dark at the lights. The second is the knowledge of your own body; you learn to hear its sound.

Snake Sisters

But if she brings home a man to marry— But if she makes him her family— But if she brings a man into their house before they have even painted the walls, hinged the doors, if she brings him in, and she becomes they, and they sleep, and they sleep, and *she* hears them through the walls— If it is night, if its edges are like teeth— If *she* lays next to the wall— If *she* walks to the kitchen to pour the pu-er and the slivered leaves are caught, stuck to the sides, and the night is howling, hollowing, and her toes are touching the unswept floor— If *she* says not a word— If the days are long, and the nights are long, and the fruit is rotted on the inside, and the wood chips are curling, the tiles cracked, and *she* says not a word— If one day, or one night, it happens unexplained, a tilt of the light, a slit of the sky, and the light is lower, louder, and one day or one night, they becomes she— If he has not disappeared but is not the point of her body, if he is one shape and she is another, if they becomes she, and so she, and *she*— If *she*— If *she* and the color through the window like bitter grapefruit, and the rind of it rinsed all round the walls—

Chang 'E

Because at that moment she understood: if daylight were a way to clarify the world, to ground it more clearly in everything *with* and *under*, then a woman who is compared to the moon has no wish to be closer to such a solar circumference but instead falls farther and father until sleep is no longer an absence but something to mottle your eaves and make them blink.

Goddess Tin Hau

Hours later, there are little tremors in the street, earthquakes you would barely notice, a tiny shivering of the ground. Restless,

I am planning my next move. In between two planes, I do not know what is right. In between two states, a wave is like a tremor. It isn't enough

to say, *we're all underwater* or *my skin is slowing*, but rather give me something hearty, an ocean fever to break between my teeth.

Nü Wa

Beating very hard, taking deep breaths, carving small homes

to be again instantly swallowed up, the sea was preparing for the body of a woman. Morning tide. Where algae has found some rocks. The body, she knows, might be represented by a series of hanging parachutes, little wombs

blooming like upturned jellyfish, falling toward the sky, or catching the rain. Her belly

carrying an ocean. In the forest someone has constructed a tiny home made of castaway textiles and market plastics which are held together by string. She thinks of a woman as a stitching of nests made of twine, twigs, yarn, and patches of cotton: each is a small home, a womb, a boat.

Chang 'E

A girl is a house her ancients build. A girl is a house inside a house. A girl is a house before she knows it. She notices the house, she says, *a house*. She says, *where is my rock?*

A home is not a home until you build it. Until you find what you can, scraps of geography that belong in your hands: ragweed, globe, oxalis:

A man on a roof is not resolving the sky-light; a woman on the ground is not waiting for him to be done. She is listening for that ever so tiny gap between the locust's hum when the sound of it wounds the air.

Nü Wa

Then, to be in the dirt, on one's knees, digging for a wayward echo, or to cover a long forgotten stone. To hide or to shelter? One must loosen the soil to make room. A seed must first split open. What do an egg, a tree, and a tempest have in common? Each is a mirror.

Snake Sisters

So we built a house in the woods. So we gathered twigs, bamboo, hemp. So we stitched a quilt from my dress, her nightsleeve, flower and cotton, and hung it down from a tree. So we stuck this rock, here, and said, do not move, little roof. So we pulled some twine and made a braid, so we laid out lines of sticks and sprigs, so we wound it under and over, again. So we tied it all together. We tied it all in a gather and propped it up for a wall. So the woods were damp, muddy leaves, and the trees were coarse and musk. So she said to tether this plastic bag, a ware for the weather, some string and a hook. We took long strands and lay out a grid, a knot at the node, and, okay, a betel nut. *Figure 1 is a vessel made of black hair and bark*. If I knit and form tiny baskets, pinecones, hives, *will you hang them on the wall*? I said an array of mute-colored structures. These structures of wildness curved into my hand. So I said, *the body is a stranger; there is always something hidden; we are haunted by the surfaces we know are there.*

Chang 'E

The earth-moon transfer orbit is a shadow-past

the longest. It holds in the sides cut away from the curve. It is a minute and lets out through the blight. *Due to the influence of the atmospheric,*

we must adjust our reckoning.

Snake Sisters

After that, I slept beneath the house, listening to the murky underpinnings of movement. After that, I paused for the drainage behind the walls, the rainwater on the roof. After that, I saw a home by the river slowly submerged, and I moved to the corridor to be filled. After that, a gruesome body

grows prescient, and it is all I can do to keep it in place. After that, I wake in the middle of the night, limbs burning in their casing. After that, a movement to sear the air, and I want to let it go like a kite. I cannot predict where all the singed pieces will land.

Nü Wa

And in between there was a moment, before the waters had receded completely, but no longer the world a massive sea, when nothing was as it should be: mountain summits partway recovered but newly interpreted in a state of suspended turmoil; beached land animals, sea creatures renamed as broken pebbles on the basin floor; electrical lines now entrenched roots; roots in the trees, the redwoods a swamp, the desert a beach, and everything half see-through in a humid sheen. The moment was sheathed in tenuous moisture. Rather than sewing up a heavenly hole, rather than gathering earth, grass and willows to weave a dam, she places one foot on blurry ground and the other is unseen. What did she expect, her body transfixed, her organs brimming, caught in the upturned fibers of an ancient tree. She stills hers breath, a feverish hum, *this is how the earth comes unsettled.* It was the old objects of the world, now drained, brief and eternal standstill of a half-sunk world, half-rebirthed.

Goddess Tin Hau

She walked to the edge of the water, unshored

her dress. The rain left angry veins in the dirt. The waves hungered, the horizon effaced. Either the sea stopped abruptly, or it continued unknowingly into the atmosphere. Each wave's tumult birthed out of an unknown source. Afterward, all they wanted was a hero; but what she wanted were broken seashells, abodes brought in by the sea, shipwrecked, half-buried in muddy embankments. In the end, which will it be? Her fingernails, the color of sea bream, at the water's ledge.

Chang 'E

If I can circle the island twice. If I can nurture my sutures toward and around this heavy-eyed mineral at eye-level. If I can plunge even as I levitate. If I can pay homage to my misshapen hour. If I can catch this beetle with my bare hands, as if something tender, If I can say, *a dream is a language half-forgotten or half-remembered.* If I can say, *I have forgotten my [   ], a lump of clay,* or, at best, *once known.* If I can watch this line of ghosting trees inside a swarming cloud, say, *the interval between borders* because that is the one *most free.*

Goddess Tin Hau

In the end, it is this she returns to, again and again: the bird biting down on a twig, the crab digging a hole. On the beach she realizes there are several of these spidery creatures: tiny translucent bodies fluttering across the sand. They rush and run sideways when they think she is not looking. Appearing and disappearing out of the underground. And now even her aloneness feels triumphant. For it is not the loneliness from before, when the view from her window felt like the earth at an edge both cavernous and eschewing, but instead, now, it is her own world holding her clearly. Now she walks through the tunnel with colorful tiles, turning left and right until she is at the edge of the water, and she can feel it like a celibate wind sweeping her hair upward and holding it there. She walks into town and is surrounded.

Chang 'E

It was a slow

departure. It stayed within this orbital plane, and it aimed at a
point in the plane. This region, about four distances "down

sun." The geometry was mostly shadowed. The uneven gravity
will have a heavier influence. Instead of "orbiting," "landing,"
"returning"

: *captured by* the moon, *when it reaches* the moon, *away from* the
moon.

Goddess Tin Hau

I was always afraid, she will say to them, her garments weighted with moisture, leaking damp shadows on the ground. Salt flakes off her skin like fish scales. They will offer her oranges, peaches, bowls of rice. Then to herself, as she turns away and slips a round fruit into her pocket, like a recitation of childhood rhymes or plaintive prayer: *when the rains recede, all that is left are women and their homes, women and their bodies, women and their aloneness.*

Nü Wa

To think of the world as a series of doors, to consider not walking through. Everything covered in a succulent haze, a cloud of droplets through which to peer and be. With a boat, I can wait and watch some very big sky as if pouring over, observing the line between cloud and storm, a mercurial spreading of eventide. With a boat, I can keep a surface, shifting or not; I can keep a world

under. Here is the part one always forgets to recall: it was my wayward cloud, my movement that made the storm gather; I buried a tooth under a mound and the largest mountains crumbled. To remain still: to be flanked by fear, absent of want, to hold out for something better. I will wait to want the sky settling down, I want to watch the sky taking root.

Chang 'E

For the house she is building: lingers, lulls, waits. As if unable, or unwilling, to look backward, forward. It wants to carve a space. Something may exist in it.

{ INTERLUDE } : WEATHER REPORTS

i.

Sometimes when the fog used to roll in and blur the ocean outside our window, I would think of all the women who fell into the sea. Women with pockets scarred with rocks, women who walked with a lingering footing, women who made little tents by the shoreline because they were waiting for some larger shadow. We go away, and we return. Or we go away. Once in our home together I woke in the middle of the night because the ambulance sirens sounded to me like the cries of a hundred birds, or bodies in turmoil, and I thought how I knew they were headed in the direction of the ocean, which at this hour would have been pitch-black, how they would have had to know where the waves were only and first by hearing it. So that outside the window when a flat cape of sky that was really a cloud began to detach from the horizon, I remembered the beach in dark hours: we sat in the debris of thousands of years of erosion, of water breaking up rock. The water was in the air.

ii.

If I were to put an ocean between us, if I were to say it begins, the relationship between body and landscape, *then it is possible one may never know how it ends. Like a woman poised toward the moon, unraveling some long-hidden thread, I may find that the land has crevices, spaces to excavate and mar with water.*

{ IV } : LOVE LETTERS

Arrivals

The sky is a moor

.

& from the airplane window,
bristling clouds in place of trees.
Instead of roads made of dirt,
currents of air.
Instead of you, the ground

.

ascending.

.

First night: monsoon.
Thunder & lightning

.

crack open the hills, every small place

.

lightens & darkens by the hour.
My neighbor appearing twice
on her roof to take in
the laundry; everything inside me
is drenched. The air
all sticky & at night I dream

.

of the earth as a tin
can filled with rocks.

.

First night: Ma On Shan, shadows of
mountains sleeping like gods.
We dragged suitcases along
unkempt grounds & passed a wet
parking lot where tiny unseen
frogs were emitting long, low sounds
like fog horns. I kept thinking
the word *bulbous*.

.

This did not yet fit

.

into a frame: You kissed me goodbye,
the sun at an apex, the air
conditioning at HKG on low.
I was crying on the ground
& my skin was sweating.
Let us say the ground was sounding
an alarm. Let us say the airplanes
were not just background
noise. Your hand
in my stringy hair, your promise
to visit, but by then the hills
will be thick, the nights over-

.

turning. A moon that spreads
the length of a year.

.

I could call it *Steps*
for Crossing the Ocean.

.

An absence: When I
was an infant my mother
told me I was born falling
from the sky. For years
I heard the wind tunneling

.

in my ears: a bruise spreading.

Myth-Making (I)

Let us say
I fell from the sky

Let us say one night I reached

around my back & could feel
the place where something had been
severed. I would always

.

try to name it.

.

An elliptical orbit :
so that I could return

to you later : how you
couldn't have known
I would want

to linger : how this
didn't mean I was not always
wishing for home.

.

I do not attempt
to cover it. In the streets
of Mong Kok & Wan Chai, I wear
thin cotton dresses & shirts
with low backs. In the crowds
I blend in. Nobody notices

my round wounds.

Nobody tries to lend me
an arm. Halfway up
the Peak, I rest my shoulder
blades against the largest
banyan tree.

.

Yesterday I walked
to the harbor being given
over to the sky. I wrote
in a letter, *I'm noticing
things again, what everyone
else already knew, how I
can always tell when
it is five o'clock
because the light
changes.*

List of Everything I Will Need

2 red pillows. A set of green bedsheets. Hot water bottle for the winter. Dehumidifying packets for the summer. 1 teapot, 1 cup, 1 plate, 1 bowl. An extra bowl for noodles. 1 frying pan, 1 pot, 1 small rice cooker. Chopsticks. Cooking utensils. Water canister. Laundry clips for hanging. A plastic bin for washing leafy vegetables.

Month 1-2

I had forgotten

how to name

.

A vowel, an orchid, this knotted tree.

.

A year

.

meant for century-old sounds :
for Tai Tam Road : for fishing towns
a boat-ride away : childhoods and
my wetted shadow : for
immigrant returns, anonymity
in a crowd, an exhale that tells me
I had once been holding
my breath : a year

for braiding the air
in an order only I could tell :

.

In the reckless heat
of the afternoon & my waning

grief I sat for hours in between
library shelves, reading children's
tales on the floor. In my notebook: *I am
a child who waits for the waters to rise
until they cover the ancient city as I sit
in my hollowed gourd. Yesterday I planted*

the thunder god's tooth. I was
carving a space
for the earth to tremble.

.

So I took the darkness

wandering around Star Ferry pier.
The air was settling me in.
Grandfathers fishing with long skinny poles
& hanging blue lightbulbs:
little eerie globes.
I want to tell you the whole night

was like this: nothing happening &

everything inside me
I felt along my spine.

In Which the City-Island Is

1: a mouthful of stars & a crescent 2: at the top of a marginal Sea 3: wavering dimensions

of child memories 4: staircase at the farthest edge, immediately beyond which sweltering 5: wild vegetation 6: three little rowboats roofed by plastic tarps 7: heart-sized bauhinia leaf pinned to the sidewalk after rainfall 8: outlying islands & those

9: unnamed 10: Mid-Autumn Festival, the city cast in billowy lanterns 11: remembrance of ferry transits, wooden ridges under foot 12: network of footbridges, tunnels, above-ground walkways 13: escalators up the mountain 14: smell of heat gone rancid, stale sewer water 15: tumult of hawker stalls & at night a street of claypot rice 16: stormclouds,

floating typhoon shelters, 17: The Walled City 18: rooftop houses 19: tiled ground, tiled buildings, tiled walls

20: red minibus to Qian Shui Wan 21: tower of buns underneath the field lights & 22: people climbing 23: dragon boats like long skating insects 24: packets of fish, dried scallops 25: sometimes a fragment I want to leave silent, a way of keeping 26: things untouched 27: gifts of *zong zi*, wrapped in leaves

28: like bandages 29: reservoir, catchwater 30: the letters G & H 31: how everything on Podium Two, still an intimate wilderness, a place for hiding, high walls 32: & abandoned corners 33: hillsides, mountains, ledges, inclines 34: necessitating a haphazard interconnectedness of myriad staircases, platforms, 35: alleys, pathways 36: like a nest 37: of some sort

Sleep Notes

To sleep fitfully
I wake in the middle of the night
to a too-hot room, my thin sheet bunched to the side.

.

I sleep next to the mountains
in the middle of the bed feeling the emptiness
on both sides.

.

Bed level with the window, window the span of the wall,
so I can see how far up I am
from the lights of others, how wide the mountains
spread around me.

.

If you were here, I might sleep
to the side, pressed
against the glass.

.

Night breaks: I hear a cricket
or small creature rustling around, but I find nothing
in the pile of clothes & plastic bags.

.

Unable to sleep, I wake early, open the curtains next to my
body. I lie, watching clouds travel at their own pace across the eyelid
of hills. If you were here I would wonder what it would be to leave
a warm body in the cool hours, to take a walk as the sun is still half-
under the earth, call it an act of courage.

.

Body, I lied, pretending it
was all you needed. Body, I am treading.

What Is Between Us (I)

1

Water, water

2

miles and miles

of oceanic trenches, igneous rock, the North Equatorial Current

3

Sky and sky and sky

at night

rocky outlines, the last of the light, the milky water

humming of insects so loud at dusk as if thick trees thrashing in a wild

4

summer storm

5

If I am forgetting your body

Instead:

the curve of hill outside my window:

a point at which the green mouth trespasses

a low-hanging cloud

my body

6

coming up for air

7

If it is true that I left you

It is also true that I will one day return

Tiny Love Letters

Flooded trees

.

Illegal architecture

.

Aerial maps
of salt fields,

a catalog
of linguistic archives.

Between the pages

.

is a walled city
creased in grids:

.

imaginary excavations:

.

the archaeologist
who doubles

as the lover at

.

midnight.

A Record of My Wrongdoing

Agarwood, rose apple, javawood & witch-hazels, ericales (it has a milky sap) & myrtles: japanese bay trees (persea), short-flowered machilus (短花楠), cekiang machilus (長序潤楠), cinnamon trees, 木荷, 罗浮栲, japanese camellia kissi, cleyera, magnolia fordiana (龙楠树), chinese banyan, chinese laurel (salamander tree, currant tree), 黄桐, 九节, abacus plant, camphor tree, baeckea, fried egg plant (I always called it egg flower), oblong-leaf litsea, india hawthorn, red melastome, embelia vine, chinese sweetspire, 降真香, ivy tree, chinese sumac, yellow cow wood

October

Tung Chung, an island
made of sea combs
umbrella ferns & lung-
shaped leafs

.

Twisted plant fibers

.

I would walk to the end
of each pier, as far as I could
to be as close as I could to
being surrounded.
At the bottom
of the mountain, layered
in vegetation, I would fall
down bus steps where forest
turned to beach, only
to be met with a family of
meandering cows

.

Mong Fu Shek on a cliff,
her body too light
for the ground.
The smallest sister
heavy as a rock, calcifying
into the sea

.

This terrible sin:
to want an empire
for my contorted limbs.

Too late, too lush
were the low-lying
shrubs. To recall, say, *imprint:*
that is, *territory*: by & for
these bones, flesh, organs

.

These rocks comprise

weathering.
They contain fossils
such as plant remains

.

I felt like a splitting
scar between trees
spreading from head
to toe: something
to be unzipped by

.

Sometimes we begin
as flood
& gradually learn to shore.
It is the process perhaps
of looking at things
alone. Unwoven,
the body builds
an altar
loose, saturated in it

Cartography

1

rocks;

river flood plain, washed over.

tropical seashore and swamp, volcano.

2

uplift and erosion: as if these were tender
words, a lover's vocabulary. as if I were to say
arteries and veins or in this region *water-cut*

3

epistolary body

to catch all of its rain and sediment, I walked
down to the beach, tried to recall a history
of morphology, like architects
who concern themselves with rain.
salt I think is what lies at the center, a city once farms by the shore.
tide starts making its way back into the wild
between breaths, beginning at the laundry outside my window.

4

land reclamation, a project of migration. they worry
about the texture of a city underwater, but I know
a secret;

throw in a seed,
the brine will reserve my body in five successive ponds.

Myth-Making (II)

On my back, a number of doors

.

ajar. Tangles of lesions, like
overripe fruit.

.

In a far-off
village in the New Territories
the koi are jumping out
of the ponds, exposing

their oranges & pinks
to the sun &
nobody knows why.

.

On my way to a house
the directions she gives me
are these: *right at the temple,*
left at the pigs, a narrow alley,
three houses, a pond of taro plants.

.

I can see them in the mirror
when I turn. A geography

.

between my shoulders.
A reminder about tributaries

of air.

.

This is what I know: that day last year
at the aquarium, all those tall plants
suspended in water.

I had you take a picture of me
next to a starfish stuck on the glass.

.

At night I climb the fence keeping
me from an edge.
I sit above the inky sea waves. I let
my feet dangle where I cannot see.

Nighttime concrete, unkempt weeds,
flowering trees in the lamp-
light. Tiny flies biting at my ankles. I am

watching little lights trek upward,
I am watching
airplanes take to the air.

.

In the old village center
instead of fish in the pond
floating atop are three

sculptures: giant paper-boats
made with giant Chinese newspapers.
In my heart I imagine they are

.

reports on ocean
currents, how to navigate

by sunless sky.

Asterisks

1: Celestial Pole at the End of Wet Market

Here is the island made up of one large star and several infant stars gesticulating sideways.

On the first star of the island are bundles of branches like long cylindrical nests, round watermelons resting in a heap, watery compartments of prawns, shrimp, clams, and crab.

Pomelo, green guava, dragon fruit, lychee.

A dark slippery fish flopping on a soppy tile floor, slithering away from a bucket.

There are slick red buckets, wet floors overlaid with squishy rubber mats, and the smell of sea animals quietly breathing.

In the compartments full of creatures, they slosh around and there is overspill of water. The smell hangs lightly, floats heavily, mists. A man with a cigarette dangling from his lips cleans the fish on a large chunk of wood. The movement of his knife sweeping across the board causes a splash as a thick mixture of water and blood hits the floor.

On the northern end of the star, a grandmother inspects a live chicken, its feet splayed. She touches the chicken in between the middle, in the belly, where I imagine the feathers to be softest and full of air.

I wait by the nests of twigs and branches. They are not tied, because their entanglements keep them together. The sticks are meant to be added to water, my mother once told me, to make a soup with heavenly powers even she cannot justify.

2: *Childhood Amongst Green Mountains*

My first memory is always of being cocooned, stowed away.

My second is of wading through flooded platforms on the way to school, the sound of waterlogged tiles, believing mornings were supposed to be this way.

Here is the point in the night sky called *My Return to Seawater Gullies*. We are using a flashlight to locate it. Here is the window where I sit fifty-three floors above sea-level. Here are the tiny silent bodies walking across the plaza below. Here are the double-decker buses turning, children in bare feet and the eight o'clock angle, here are the cargo ships snailing their way in a silver margin that will soon appear blue. Here is the path I walk every morning, across a gray tiled bridge, where at night when I make my way back, I catch glimpses of geometry atop the foothills.

3: *Southern Asterisms*

To get to the winter morning of the southern stars, I follow the afternoon light which is casting a haze in one part of the sky. I end up on a path next to the water, where I sit on a ledge reading a book of architecture drawings as the sun begins to lower behind the mountains and the sky becomes a chilled pomelo. On the bank of rocks below me: cigarette box, bicycle tire, heap of dead leaves. A large boat in the distance blows its slow horn and several moments later, the water below my feet begins to heave, sloshing across the roughened, barnacled rocks. The sudden disturbance alarms me, and I look up until it is quiet again. Above the sea from mountain to mountain is a line of cable cars, strung lights, blinking back and forth across the horizon. I sit on the ledge, reading, until it is dark and my hands are too cold to turn the pages.

4: Star Map in a Woman's Grave

I teach myself, slowly: to hold a seeded fruit in one hand while my body creates a shadow on the ground. To trust the bus will come. To be alone in seasonal temperatures, to ride on the back of her summer bicycle through tall fields and dense foliage toward the island's ferry. To believe in the strength of her legs. To build an exposed beam.

5: Snake's Tale: Vermillion Bird

For months I walked through the city, counting in my head, *The star is a city of windows. The star is a city of tiles. The star is a city of alleyways...* I took the labyrinth of moving stairways through the middle of the city, passing multi-levels of restaurants, fabric shops, hair salons, residences, signs clamoring in a haphazard landscape. I walked up and down steep hills and often saw the next hour coming around the street corner or the plenitude of flat rooftops, laundry lines, vegetable gardens at the narrowest edge. I loitered around temples, waited for the spicy aroma to settle in my hair, caught the ashes falling onto my shoulder.

What Is Between Us (II)

1

Here is a hole:

2

You call me at my night
hours, say: *I am starting to feel like we are not*

3

married. The ocean multiplies.

4

In the evening I lie on the bed, imagining what it looks like
between our sleeping bodies.
At some point in the middle

5

the view would be of only water, crests of waves
in all directions.
Or:

6

If we might spread a paper map covered in gridded blue
beneath us on one bed, a thick crinkling under our weight. And
suspended from above

7

a cross-oceanic frame between

8

two points.

Body & Landscape

It begins *the relationship between body and landscape*, or *how to love the lover's body*, otherwise known as *landscape as lover*. Also included are *heart, nighttime escalators, green hills* (you knew this), *how walking is keenly felt, anticipate*, and *gingerly*.

What Grows

Wind / tunnels, holloways / animal tracks / what churns like
spoiled skin / a portrait of watercolor / islands, briny / & festering /

When the sores on my back leak liquid / I peddle toward Tai Mei
Tuk like I am / swimming / rice fields, simmering wetlands, bodies
of women / ankle-deep /

Half-way / across the dam / weather systems / descending / the
weight of / a spine-shaped cloud / scales scraped against the knife

Creation Myth

Women of
Sai Kung
have fallen
onto sea
debris
in order to
love their
bodies more
Untethered
the bodies
of the seven
sisters
are fermenting
rock-grit
siltstone
shale
Let me quarry
the hemispheric
drift
Let me curdle
the nightful
home

How to Love the Lover's Body

1

Half-water, half-flesh.

2

Fish dumplings, egg pancakes, and other pocket-like concoctions.

3

Ten fish drying in the sun, a laundry line of newly salted linen. Mobiles of dried squid. If I were to keep an audio diary, it would begin with three measures of that old melody played out in the underpassage. When I emerge, it is already night.

4

In the spring, I slung two plastic oranges onto a banyan tree and wished to never return home. That is to say, I always knew when the day was about to end by the quality of the sky. This is the beating heart of an already-dead fish, but then again I was always ready to let the landscape replace our bodies.

5

The researcher asked each of her subjects to draw a map of their neighborhood, so that she could see the land through their eyes. We are always measuring ourselves against the rocks that carry us. I wanted to see the hills as if it were a wash basin, the color not unlike bathtub water. I am not sure how to say that I have found something to cradle in this place, and yet here on a rock, my head tilts a few degrees south. Perhaps I am looking across the distance at your body sleeping in the dark. Perhaps the distance is what I have found.

What Is Between Us (III)

1

To love the sky between us

2

Where mine meets yours, a peak
to form a roof

3

For a year I watched the atmosphere shift over the island, so I
could know

I felt the boundaries slip and I also felt it orb

To slow an apocalypse I might spread my arms

4

How to mark negative space

The width of a stormfall

If light is scarce, I will name myself in the dark

5

To pull up from the roots, the body
cannot help but find new directions

Distortion allows us to recognize

6

A person sitting on the ground with mounds of salt
charting a labyrinth to capture their grief

7

So there can be a journey home—

8

My mother who gave me a lullaby, *fall into a well of ghosts*

My mother, generous with darkness
but never how to waylay the moon
In her wisdom I slept all my rivers, wrested all
my ground until my ground

9

was neck-deep

10

At the bus stop one summer evening
Something to take you away—

11

This is how the ocean grows:

Every night I reach toward my recesses

Presents I Do Not Send You

Barefoot in my apartment
my heels & toes pick up
dust, bits of thread, dirt.
A constellation I might place
into an envelope gently.

.

You are probably sleeping now.

.

Humidity encircling the city in
sedate drowning. Dampened sidewalks.
Umbrellas rotating in a crowd
from above.

.

A surprising feeling: desire
for some dimension
of earth, whose perimeters
are not yet measurable.

.

In the evening in the rainy
alley reflecting the tarp of the watchmaker stall,
a girl I hardly know: *it is those slippery
moments* & then she stops. Or
I have forgotten what is next.
It is the fact of the word *slippery,*
that is how I knew.

Betrayals

To return to me now
you must also leave. A moveable ghost

in place of solid ground.
After you have come & gone, my breathing
returns to its natural rhythm instead of
something caught in my throat.

At night in bed next to the mountains
I resented the space you
took up. I resented the way you touched
me, how your mouth stayed silent, how you

plucked at the growths on my back but did not
give them vowels.

.

In the living room I hear the faint sound of water

inside a bathtub from the unit above me.
In the afternoon it is the sound of piano, but at night
I can hear water moving.

I tell someone, *it is like being underwater.*
He says, *you lie.*

.

Inside the cold planetarium
I remove my shoes, dripping
from the monsoon season. I take notes in the darkness
to later make out the letters. Later: a small
self-contained ecosphere, steeped in too much algae.
Once, we'd climbed a tower & you said, *you can see the ocean;*
I said, *no, you can see the moon on the water.*

.

Years ago I paused, astounded to find
a pinecone I took home had expanded
in an hour of hot sun. It had escaped
the container in which I'd laid it.
Later, I returned to find it
small, once again.

.

On the smallest island where I took you by ferry,
there was not much there: a temple for the sea,
two tin-colored fish tied to a clothes hanger,
elephant leafs to dwarf your head.

.

The anticipation of returning
causes a strange density

to settle in my chest. I am restless,

I sleep at odd hours, take frantic walks
& spend all my time in MTR stations,
on trams, inside tunnels, up &
down escalators, between pedestrian bridges.

.

I sit at home in front of a fan, sweating.
I keep listening for the hemispheres to tilt.

Unwashed dishes in the sink & I am poised
for punishment, listening to a song I haven't heard
in years, sweating, full of guilt for forgetting
to turn off the air conditioner when I went for groceries.

.

Or: if I were to make a constellation
out of string & wire, hanging above my bed.
When I look up, I would see what you see.
All these months, I haven't yet spied

the stars out at night. They are lost
somewhere over the Pacific.

What the Body Knows

1

When we married, I thought that all we needed was some light, a small bed, a place to warm our rice. We didn't talk about space or boundaries, how much we would each inhabit, how to determine what lines or where. Now between hemispheres there is an undefined vastness. *It feels like floating*, and by that you mean there is nothing to tether us, nothing we can hold onto to make us whole. *Here is a space*, I want to say to you, while holding out my cupped hands. The space feels like water the color of lukewarm milk.

2

I tried to draw thick lines, again and again, around my body in various orientations, as if in that way I could learn its shape.

3

What does the land sound like to you? She was talking about signs and typefaces, but I have always wondered what it would be like to carry a sound recorder with me, a chronicle of my movements in space, turning it on, shutting it off, collecting pieces of the day here and there.

4

I imagined my body as I slept—the light and dimness of the city below me, contoured by geography, falling across my uncovered legs, my closed eyes. *We sleep*, I said, *so our bodies can be alone.* If you were here, either I would sleep with my back toward you, or I would spend all night cleaving, my body reaching out for yours.

5

I would peel a single grape and serve it to you whole. How does one measure it? It is not nothing; there is an ocean. And the ocean is a real space: it has ridges, depths, the largest stretch of mountains on the earth's surface.

6

It is difficult to know how attuned our bodies are to the position, the frequency, of one another. Like wavelengths, one is at the crest and I am at the ridge, but it is possible that asleep, we are breathing at the same rate.

7

In the month before I leave, my body begins to break down in small and strange ways: first, my nose ceases to be a passageway for air, my voice takes on a low, nasal quality; then my ears plug inexplicably, even as I sleep; finally, the world will seem to spin too quickly each time I lay my head down or sit up again. I will spend one night crying, and another morning I will wake up angry, kicking at the covers.

.

I am here & you are there & we are separated
by ocean, hemispheres,
topography, solitude,
my attempts at courage, your steady beat.

I imagine a red string tied around my foot, running across the
globe, ending
around your ankle.

.

In the local tongue, I am treading water.

My back in the heat shuttering open and closed: teeth chattering.

Your environment shapes your language. My body: an arrow, a curve, a hyphen.

Myth-making (III)

When my back begins to drip red—red streaks in the shower,
red shadows on the rocks at Cheung Sha beach, red droplets
on the wet market floor where the fish have not yet been slit,
the chickens not yet stripped, red stains on the chairs at Tsui
Wah like ink stamps—then I know there is no turning back.
A red puddle may appear as blood but in reality is fluid wrung
from insect wings taking their very first breath. An insect in
a cocoon keeps all of its materials but changes the ordering
of its structures. It keeps all of its materials, but the cocoon
surrounding the insect breaks. If the cocoon is skin. If the
cocoon is flesh. If the cocoon is another shadow it has wrapped
around itself. A bystander, a casualty.

{ V } : FROM THE VOICE OF THE
LADY IN THE MOON

CHANG 'E:

Some mornings when I wake, I know that in my sleep I have been weaving a net around my body, like fish hefted in from ocean waves, or a way to catch a fallen starling. I never wanted a world clear as ether; instead I wanted a faraway sky to press my body up against, a boundary ever to push away. On the stairs as I made my way down to the ground, I saw that there were moths of all sizes stuck to the wall: small and large but always flat, as if cut carefully from an old paper bag. All day I kept hearing metaphors: migrating salmon, nocturnal tides, the return of planetary bodies. When I say moon, I almost never mean the moon. When I say moon, I mean the light of the sky is about to disappear behind the beached ocean and I cannot hold it anymore, it is spilling between my fingers. When I say to you it is a strange moon day, you should know I mean the unsettling of our underbellies, strewn across such rigorous comings and goings.

CHANG 'E:

If I were more careful, the dishes would not be chipped, the tub not a discolored rust. At various times during the day I find the light too meager, too hesitant, or otherwise possessed. I move from room to room as if to monitor my body's absorption of external particles, but really I am drawn to what I cannot name, the slant of light a brief home for this patch of skin. Outside, I can see clusters of sturdy green leaves emerging from the underground, trembling and waving recklessly, as if prickled by a self-assured wind. Underwater, their movements would resemble swimming. If he eclipses me in my own house; if he haunts my movement like a shadow to ground an unknown desire; if he notices habitual wounds, household failures, but says nothing—then I will plant a garden of creeping winter, walking onion, orris root, their stalks able to reach sky-shaped distances, their leaves unafraid to impress on the skin. I am grateful for the odd unruly pine, its limbs so sprawling it cannot be held by a metal wire. I am grateful for tree bark that flakes into moths, for dandelion spores that swim upward straight through earthly branches, never caught, never landing.

CHANG 'E:

In the avoidance of all things
earthly, I hoped for some
clouds with which to eclipse
the ground. I monitored the
low sound of the earth splitting
instead of the depth of cavity it
promised to carve. There is salt
where salt does not belong, and
a wound grows. It is thrush
with branches I nevertheless
tend. If I keep the succulent in
the sun where its leaves turn
redder still, there might still be
something left over for me.

CHANG 'E:

Inside my dilapidated house, the shape
of my disarray is a crack in the flooring, a
slim panel of wood raised slightly ajar.
On the other side of the wall in the
exterior, the house is torn, catching
rainwater in its side until mold begins to
spread. Even an intruder casts a shadow
as slight as a layer of dust under the bed,
even an intruder can awaken something
lying low underneath. We pretend that a
body loves a person, but a body loves a
ghost. A body loves the house. A body
loves the moon.

CHANG 'E:

Ever transiting
toward some old
nocturnal light,
we pretend it is
not in vain. We
are all night-
ridden insects.
Unstuck, it waves
aflicker—

CHANG 'E:

So that the grounding beneath my feet is nowhere found, and there is nothing by which to base everyday decisions like, *Is it right to bend a little into the window light?* or *What is the last thing I am able to say aloud before it becomes a secret?* Suddenly the same everyday questions are left dangling, unhinged, and one can only move into them as if into a dark closet. So there is nothing to be done except to build my house over there, where the water is deep and the rocks obscured in seaweed. I walk across meters of shattered and crushed shells, balancing across hard stones where I can, to avoid breaking life.

CHANG 'E:

If I can feel such a wound, then perhaps I might know where my body exists in a room, where it begins and ends, where it comes into contact with a world on fire. If it is possible to love a person with every hair on your head, every prickle of your skin: it is possible to love a person imperfectly. What do we honor with this unobscured movement in the dark? I inspect unlit corners, examine forgotten cracks behind the furniture, as if these might be places for a tiny house to exist. Here is a space not to give a noise but to feel where the body hinges. So in the evening when I ride the rickety bus across town, I might turn to the woman next to me, as if bespectacled, *you are not bowled over by the wind*. My own mode of navigation, he says, like holding an umbrella sideways.

CHANG 'E:

Until one night in my sleep, I followed the intruder home. As if to admit a part of my body lived there, a small circular table, the sound of distant traffic like an afternoon nap. *Here is an eave for every hard crescent unborn*, I say with folded hands. Piles of unwashed dishes, heaps of soiled clothes, a disheveled rug. What belongs to us more: our home or our strangers? An intruder can be the imprint of foreign weather, a space I keep ghostly at the side; it is an absence, a trace, something I bring back to the bedroom after peering into unlit alleyways as if they were the sky. At the intruder's house, the light is a small, dirty glow. I stare into the hollow round of a yellowed glass jar until it fills my field of vision.

CHANG 'E:

What does it mean for a woman to think of her
face occluded, her hand enclosed inside a another
hand even as she angles herself toward an invisible
space? They tell me: the moon is not the moon
but the sun reflecting off dark spaces and odd
shapes. I say: the moon is a body I cannot yet
name. If the purpose of a map is to show us the
way home, then what I want is a navigational
marker that spreads outward, or deepens in a
location I can begin with my own two sticks and a
handful of pebbles.

CHANG 'E:

Here is how I make my body
mine, that is, in between the
small talk he does not touch me
but instead touches all the things
that have just touched me: my
sweater sleeve, my bottle of
water. The word *appendage* or
hinge. A boundary washes up on
the shore, again and again,
erasing and appearing in the
blink of an eye.

CHANG 'E:

She might be hurt, she might be
tricked. How do we know which
pain is necessary, and which we
inflict on ourselves? Someone
fears boredom, another unties
boundaries. I am alternately
bewildered and longing. Once
upon a time, a girl could not
look at the ocean. She held her
shadow selves at bay, cast them a
secret into the kelp. Test the
water and she will shake, her
muscles on the verge of some
unraveling panic. When I sleep
next to the sea, encircled by
smooth white stones, the center
of the body is never merely
corporeal but the longing to
hold a wave or at least to feel my
arm extended outward. If I am
afraid of the ocean, then I will
take a boat out to the middle of
the breaks. I want to root a
garden into a home while also
being carried out by the current.
These are contradictions we
want to find essential, to say,
moon, here I come.

CHANG 'E:

Let us say the moon is a house I have not yet
learned. *Moon* as if it were lover. Let us say
she, let us say hers. Let us say how *the body's
desire is a longing for home.*

CHANG 'E:

We remind ourselves how moths navigate: when light is obscured, their bodies are drawn through constellatory fields of magnetic orbit. I move slowly through the house, dragging dust and light. In the morning when I wake the whales are spread along the beach. In the morning the whales are swimming inshore and southward, slow and disorganized. The reports say, *two dozen stranded themselves*. We are speaking of one thing, and we are speaking of many.

CHANG 'E:

We learned this lesson from the whales: the larger the gap between bodies, the more satisfying it is when we come close. Or: Having spent years like an insect inside a walnut shell the only way I knew how, it is possible that one day I might push outward, clear the atmosphere around me. A shell can be a slow grave from which one is trying to wake. *The house is leaning to the right; catch it, if you will.* The wings of a moth are thin as paper, the world is always turning over in the dark, and out there in the night the whales are ever pushing outward, in search of something that will hold their attention, keep their heft.

CHANG 'E:

It begins with the house —
small cracks, unswept corners,
inconspicuous messes — and
then I am knocking into
things. Until one day piles of
paper scatter the air, and dust
atop the door frames blows
sideways. All things eventually
come down. In between
suspensions, I walk out to
meet the intruder, as if
something might be lost in the
rain gutter, the detritus, in the
downdraft of inclement
weather.

CHANG 'E:

Or: Where do I end, and my body underwater begins? She said, *there is value in knowing our floor*, and I understood this to mean that sometimes the ground is a boundary that holds us: we cannot fall any further. I took this to mean, the ground is a surface that spreads forever. Attuned to the rifts of daily movement, one cannot help but begin to notice the grime growing underneath the faucet, the paint chips collecting at the hinge of the door. One becomes sensitive to the way morning cloud cover settles in the heart like a body yawning for some onerous distance. A string of good weather brings sun and blue skies, but sometimes I remember the roof is misaligned.

CHANG 'E:

To unbuild in order to build; I kept myself empty for
something to fill. But in the meantime, a missing
doorknob, the splintered chair, weather seeping in
through unseen cracks. Outside the bathroom window,
a layer of the exterior had peeled and was flapping
violently in the wind, a sound I mistook for a bird
seeking flight.

CHANG 'E:

A chrysalis is an envelope of earthly hues, raw green, wrinkly dried brown, seeded vessels like leguminous plants. Instead of the transformation of their wings, now the rows of sleeping pods. *Instar*, and I am holding a word of celestial materials, ready to make a world apart. Sky and sea, speckled with gold, and empty ones, thin layers of lip skin, translucent, slit open. Inside the envelope: decomposition, disintegration, destruction. The structures are carried in the dissolution. The body holds knowledge as if it were a horoscope, an omen, an intuition of atmospheric currents to come.

CHANG 'E:

If the sky like the body of a sick
child: swollen, damp, sweating.
If it fermented overnight into
something monstrous, held in
the throat, tentative where the
air stretched tenuously. If it was
humid with heat finally broken
into cooling, potent with the
strangeness of a night that had
tossed and turned half-
consciously, tumultuously, a
foreign window half open, the
sound of a fan whirring. If a
lump in the corner fomented,
gathered mucus. If *something
monstrous in form: meshes.* If in
the morning, all kinds of
unusual debris: coffins, boats,
species of turtles, an ancient
canoe, the body of a sharp-
toothed eel.

CHANG 'E:

So I let the ocean grow. Never mind my
elusive limbs, my body spread in mass
directions. I found a crack and hid inside
in order to be cradled. As if to say, *weather
me*. As if I did not know the lull of the
tide, I waited for the night to carry all
things home. There is fluid in the wings,
and I am letting rain collect in forgotten
corners. Give me a boat to fill with water,
sew into my pocket a parachute of rocks
and shells. I wanted the sky and settled for
an expanse in which to immerse. Cover me
then with things that sleep: earth-
toned habitat, half-hemispheres, the eye of
a storm.

CHANG 'E:

And what of the house made of ruins?
Thousands of years later it will be overrun with
trees growing into walls, thick roots upturning
stones; a tiny body might wander through piles
of rubble and loosened fragments with careful
steps and a lungful of debris. Inside my house,
the air is subtle with tender misgivings I hold as
if something to safeguard against an ancient and
tired wind. Inside the house, the salt is spilt, and
I am keeping my fingers numb in case the stove
catches fire. I am watching it rust, believing that
water is pure and does no one harm. If I were
honest, I would offer to more than a ghost my
mutterings of lists and duties. *A stranger, a
disturbance, so I held my ear to the ground, my
mouth to the sky.* In the morning when I woke,
my teeth felt cold and light fell away from their
appropriate objects.

CHANG 'E:

If I had wanted to leave the whole structure behind, I would have. In the building filled with various histories, I saw that objects were hanging from the ceiling or fixed to the ground. They were kept on shelves, attached to walls. I wandered through centuries of relics, and in the room made of windows with a river, I wondered at what point do we become strangers to ourselves, do the distances recall a void that cannot be crossed. I divide the body, I divide the heart. In trying to be a savior, I am uprooted. I cut an A-frame into the wall: *a body for my home, a home for the body*. Somewhere in the weather where I am listening to the baseboard, pressed against the frame, measuring the angle of the door; somewhere in the unmooring of a new house to build, a moon to unfetter, a sky to unhold, I want to relearn him upturning that ghost, I want to mark a new map for a body opening, body holding unto its own windblown anchor.

NOTES

The book draws loosely on common Chinese folktales. Additionally, it references specific sources:

P. 17: "*She is the Moon, she is the Water, she is Cold, she is Autumn and Winter, she is the Shadows*" is from the children's book *Chinese Myths and Legends* by Philip Ardagh (Belitha, 1998).

P. 29: "*weaving, knitting, knotting*" & "*a chorus, fugue, the song cycle*" are words from Barbara Tomash's notes to me regarding the manuscript; "*a cone of salt, a way of moving around it*" & "*a place where we get to forget something, as much as remember*" are from an email sent to me by Bhanu Kapil regarding the manuscript; "*plot of light, water, house, self, space*" is transcribed from Sasha West's comments to me regarding the manuscript.

P. 43, 58, 64: These pieces manipulate language from CCTV.com.

P. 44: "*What appears to be terra firma was likely water not so long ago*" is from *Cities Without Ground* by Adam Frampton, Jonathan D. Solomon, & Clara Wong (ORO, 2012).

P. 102: The first two stanzas are based on language from *Poetics of Space* by Gaston Bachelard (Beacon, 1994).

P. 133: "*something monstrous in form: meshes*" is based on language in an email from Bhanu Kapil regarding the manuscript.

ACKNOWLEDGEMENTS

Immense gratitude to Bhanu Kapil for believing in my manuscript, and to Christian Peet and Tarpaulin Sky Press, whose books I have loved.

Thank you to the journals in which parts and excerpts first appeared: *Black Warrior Review* and *Foundry*, where it received Pushcart Prize nominations, *The Adroit Journal*, which nominated it for Best Small Fictions, *Quarter After Eight*, where it was winner of the Robert J. DeMott Short Prose Contest, *The Offing*, *Iron Horse Literary Review*, *Tupelo Quarterly*, *Hyphen*, and *Fourteen Hills*. Thank you to *BWR*, who invited me to write a craft essay for their blog, which became the prelude, and to *Poor Claudia*, who published "A Poetics of Iteration," which helped me to understand my obsessions.

I am grateful to the U.S. Fulbright program, the Bread Loaf Writers' Conference, and Kundiman for providing time and space and landscape for this project's inceptions and continuations.

Special thank you to Maude Tanswai for her beautiful cover art and to Bhanu Kapil, Barbara Tomash, and Sasha West for their particular support and for allowing me to weave in language from their luminous notes to me. Thank you to: my teachers Maxine Chernoff, Toni Mirosevich, Truong Tran; the immense women in my life who read, edited, or otherwise contributed to these pages, especially SH, JH, TH, JL, JJL, CT, MT, HVH, APW, GY, DLP, Quadrangle, all Wild Girl Poets; my family here and overseas; and the one in my heart, with whom I cross & uncross distances. Here is Audre Lorde, reminding us of *that power which rises from our deepest and nonrational knowledge...a measure between our sense of self and the chaos of our strongest feelings.*

ABOUT THE AUTHOR

Jennifer S. Cheng's hybrid collection *Moon: Letters, Maps, Poems*, was chosen by Bhanu Kapil as co-winner of the 2017 Tarpaulin Sky Book Award. Cheng is also the author of *House A*, selected by Claudia Rankine as winner of the Omnidawn Poetry Book Prize, and *Invocation: An Essay*, an image-text chapbook published by New Michigan Press. Her poetry, lyric essays, and critical writing appear in *Tin House*, *AGNI*, *Black Warrior Review*, *DIAGRAM*, *The Offing*, *Entropy*, *Jacket2*, *Guernica*, and elsewhere. She was a Fulbright Scholar in Hong Kong and received fellowships and awards from Brown University, the University of Iowa, San Francisco State University, Bread Loaf, Kundiman, and the Academy of American Poets. Having grown up in Texas and Hong Kong, she lives in San Francisco. www.jenniferscheng.com

TARPAULIN SKY PRESS

Warped from one world to another. (*THE NATION*) Somewhere between
Artaud and Lars Von Trier. (*VICE*) Hallucinatory ... trance-inducing....
A kind of nut job's notebook.... Breakneck prose harnesses the throbbing
pulse of language itself.... Playful, experimental appeal.... Multivalent,
genre-bending.... Unrelenting, grotesque beauty. (*PUBLISHERS WEEKLY*)
Simultaneously metaphysical and visceral.... Scary, sexual, and intellectually
disarming. (*HUFFINGTON POST*) Horrifying and humbling.... (*THE RUMPUS*)
Wholly new. (*IOWA REVIEW*) ....only becomes more surreal. (*NPR BOOKS*)
The opposite of boring.... An ominous conflagration devouring the bland
terrain of conventional realism.... Dangerous language, a murderous kind
... discomfiting, filthy, hilarious, and ecstatic. (*BOOKSLUT*) Creating a zone
where elegance and grace can gambol with the just-plain-fucked-up.
(*HTML GIANT*) Uncomfortably enjoyable. (*AMERICAN BOOK REVIEW*)
Consistently inventive. (*TRIQUARTERLY*) A peculiar, personal music that is
at once apart from and very much surrounded by the world. (*VERSE*) A world
of wounded voices. (*HYPERALLERGIC*) Futile, sad, and beautiful. (*NEWPAGES*)
Inspired and unexpected. Highly recommended. (*AFTER ELLEN*)

MORE FROM TS PRESS >>

STEVEN DUNN
POTTED MEAT

Co-winner, Tarpaulin Sky Book Award
Shortlist, *Granta*'s "Best of Young American Novelists"
Finalist, Colorado Book Award
SPD Fiction Bestseller

Set in a decaying town in West Virginia, Steven Dunn's debut novel, *Potted Meat,* follows a boy into adolescence as he struggles with abuse, poverty, alcoholism, and racial tensions. A meditation on trauma and the ways in which a person might surivive, if not thrive, *Potted Meat* examines the fear, power, and vulnerability of storytelling itself. "101 pages of miniature texts that keep tapping the nails in, over and over, while speaking as clearly and directly as you could ask.... Bone Thugs, underage drinking, alienation, death, love, Bob Ross, dreams of blood.... Flooded with power." **(BLAKE BUTLER, *VICE MAGAZINE*)** "Full of wonder and silence and beauty and strangeness and ugliness and sadness.... This book needs to be read." **(LAIRD HUNT)** "A visceral intervention across the surface of language, simultaneously cutting to its depths, to change the world.... I feel grateful to be alive during the time in which Steven Dunn writes books." **(SELAH SATERSTROM)**

ELIZABETH HALL
I HAVE DEVOTED MY LIFE TO THE CLITORIS

Co-winner, Tarpaulin Sky Book Award
Finalist, Lambda Literary Award for Bisexual Nonfiction
SPD Nonfiction Bestseller

Debut author Elizabeth Hall set out to read everything that has been written about the clitoris. The result is "Freud, terra cotta cunts, hyenas, anatomists, and Acker, mixed with a certain slant of light on a windowsill and a leg thrown open invite us. Bawdy and beautiful." (**WENDY C. ORTIZ**). "An orgy of information ... rendered with graceful care, delivering in small bites an investigation of the clit that is simultaneously a meditation on the myriad ways in which smallness hides power." (***THE RUMPUS***) "Marvelously researched and sculpted.... bulleted points rat-tat-tatting the patriarchy, strobing with pleasure." (**DODIE BELLAMY**) "Philosophers and theorists have always asked what the body is—Hall just goes further than the classical ideal of the male body, beyond the woman as a vessel or victim, past genre as gender, to the clitoris. And we should follow her." (***KENYON REVIEW***) "Gorgeous little book about a gorgeous little organ.... The 'tender button' finally gets its due." (**JANET SARBANES**) "You will learn and laugh .... God this book is glorious." (**SUZANNE SCANLON**)

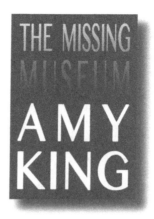

AMY KING
THE MISSING MUSEUM

Co-winner, Tarpaulin Sky Book Award
SPD Poetry Bestseller

Nothing that is complicated may ever be simplified, but rather catalogued, cherished, exposed. *The Missing Museum* spans art, physics & the spiritual, including poems that converse with the sublime and ethereal. They act through ekphrasis, apostrophe & alchemical conjuring. They amass, pile, and occasionally flatten as matter is beaten into text. Here is a kind of directory of the world as it rushes into extinction, in order to preserve and transform it at once. "'Understanding' is not a part of the book's project, but rather a condition that one must move through like a person hurriedly moving through a museum." (**PUBLISHERS WEEKLY**) "Women's National Book Association Award-winner Amy King balances passages that can prompt head-scratching wonder with a direct fusillade of shouty caps.... You're not just seeing through her eyes but, perhaps more importantly, breathing through her lungs." (**LAMBDA LITERARY**) "A visceral stunner ... and an instruction manual.... King's archival work testifies to the power—however obscured by the daily noise of our historical moment—of art, of the possibility for artists to legislate the world." (**KENYON REVIEW**)

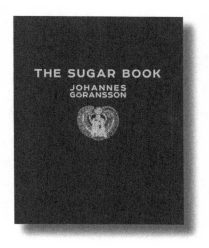

JOHANNES GÖRANSSON
THE SUGAR BOOK

SPD Poetry Bestseller

Johannes Göransson's *The Sugar Book* marks the author's third title with TS Press, following his acclaimed *Haute Surveillance* and *entrance to a colonial pageant in which we all begin to intricate.* "Doubling down on his trademark misanthropic imagery amid a pageantry of the unpleasant, Johannes Göransson strolls through a violent Los Angeles in this hybrid of prose and verse.... The motifs are plentiful and varied ... pubic hair, Orpheus, law, pigs, disease, Francesca Woodman ... and the speaker's hunger for cocaine and copulation..... Fans of Göransson's distorted poetics will find this a productive addition to his body of work". (*PUBLISHERS WEEKLY*) "Sends its message like a mail train. Visceral Surrealism. His end game is an exit wound." (*FANZINE*) "As savagely anti-idealist as Burroughs or Guyotat or Ballard. Like those writers, he has no interest in assuring the reader that she or he lives, along with the poet, on the right side of history." (*ENTROPY MAGAZINE*) "Convulses wildly like an animal that has eaten the poem's interior and exterior all together with silver." (KIM HYESOON) "'I make a language out of the bleed-through.' Göransson sure as fuck does. These poems made me cry. So sad and anxious and genius and glarey bright." (REBECCA LOUDON)

AARON APPS
INTERSEX

"Favorite Nonfiction of 2015," Dennis Cooper
SPD Bestseller and Staff Pick

Intersexed author Aaron Apps's hybrid-genre memoir adopts and upends historical descriptors of hermaphroditic bodies such as "imposter," "sexual pervert," "freak of nature," and "unfortunate monstrosity," tracing the author's own monstrous sex as it perversely intertwines with gender expectations and medical discourse. "Graphic vignettes involving live alligators, diarrhea in department store bathrooms, domesticity, dissected animals, and the medicalization of sex.... Unafraid of failure and therefore willing to employ risk as a model for confronting violence, living with it, learning from it." (*AMERICAN BOOK REVIEW*) "I felt this book in the middle of my own body. Like the best kind of memoir, Apps brings a reader close to an experience of life that is both 'unattainable' and attentive to 'what will emerge from things.' In doing so, he has written a book that bursts from its very frame." (BHANU KAPIL)

Excerpts from *Intersex* were nominated for a Pushcart Prize by *Carolina Quarterly*, and appear in *Best American Essays 2014*.

CLAIRE DONATO
BURIAL

A debut novella that slays even seasoned readers. Set in the mind of a narrator who is grieving the loss of her father, who conflates her hotel room with the morgue, and who encounters characters that may not exist, *Burial* is a little story about an immeasurable black hole; an elegy in prose at once lyrical and intelligent, with no small amount of rot and vomit and ghosts. "Poetic, trance-inducing language turns a reckoning with the confusion of mortality into readerly joy at the sensuality of living." (*PUBLISHERS WEEKLY* "BEST SUMMER READS") "A dark, multivalent, genre-bending book.... Unrelenting, grotesque beauty an exhaustive recursive obsession about the unburiability of the dead, and the incomprehensibility of death." (*PUBLISHERS WEEKLY* STARRED REVIEW) "Dense, potent language captures that sense of the unreal that, for a time, pulls people in mourning to feel closer to the dead than the living.... Sartlingly original and effective." (*MINNEAPOLIS STAR-TRIBUNE*) "A grief-dream, an attempt to un-sew pain from experience and to reveal it in language." (*HTML GIANT*) "A full and vibrant illustration of the restless turns of a mind undergoing trauma.... Donato makes and unmakes the world with words, and what is left shimmers with pain and delight." (BRIAN EVENSON) "A gorgeous fugue, an unforgettable progression, a telling I cannot shake." (HEATHER CHRISTLE) "Claire Donato's assured and poetic debut augurs a promising career." (BENJAMIN MOSER)

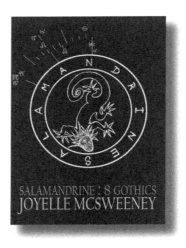

JOYELLE MCSWEENEY
SALAMANDRINE: 8 GOTHICS

Following poet and playwright Joyelle McSweeney's acclaimed novels *Flet*, from Fence Books, and *Nylund, The Sarcographer*, from Tarpaulin Sky Press, comes a collection of shorter prose texts by McSweeney, *Salamandrine: 8 Gothics*, perhaps better described as a series of formal/generic lenses refracting the dread and isolation of contemporary life and producing a distorted, attenuated, spasmatic experience of time, as accompanies motherhood. "Vertiginous.... Denying the reader any orienting poles for the projected reality.... McSweeney's breakneck prose harnesses the throbbing pulse of language itself." (*PUBLISHERS WEEKLY*) "Biological, morbid, fanatic, surreal, McSweeney's impulses are to go to the rhetoric of the maternity mythos by evoking the spooky, sinuous syntaxes of the gothic and the cleverly constructed political allegory. At its core is the proposition that writing the mother-body is a viscid cage match with language and politics in a declining age.... This collection is the sexy teleological apocrypha of motherhood literature, a siren song for those mothers 'with no soul to photograph.'" (*THE BROOKLYN RAIL*) "Language commits incest with itself.... Sounds repeat, replicate, and mutate in her sentences, monstrous sentences of aural inbreeding and consangeous consonants, strung out and spinning like the dirtiest double-helix, dizzy with disease...." (*QUARTERLY WEST*)

JENNY BOULLY
NOT MERELY BECAUSE OF THE UNKNOWN THAT WAS STALKING TOWARD THEM

"This is undoubtedly the contemporary re-treatment that Peter Pan deserves.... Simultaneously metaphysical and visceral, these addresses from Wendy to Peter in lyric prose are scary, sexual, and intellectually disarming." (*HUFFINGTON POST*) In her second SPD Bestseller from Tarpaulin Sky Press, *not merely because of the unknown that was stalking toward them*, Jenny Boully presents a "deliciously creepy" swan song from Wendy Darling to Peter Pan, as Boully reads between the lines of J. M. Barrie's *Peter and Wendy* and emerges with the darker underside, with sinister and subversive places. *not merely because of the unknown* explores, in dreamy and dark prose, how we love, how we pine away, and how we never stop loving and pining away. "To delve into Boully's work is to dive with faith from the plank — to jump, with hope and belief and a wish to see what the author has given us: a fresh, imaginative look at a tale as ageless as Peter himself." (*BOOKSLUT*) "Jenny Boully is a deeply weird writer— in the best way." (**ANDER MONSON**)

MORE FICTION, NONFICTION, POETRY
& HYBRID TEXTS FROM TARPAULIN SKY PRESS

FULL-LENGTH BOOKS

Jenny Boully, *[one love affair]**

Ana Božičević, *Stars of the Night Commute*

Traci O. Connor, *Recipes for Endangered Species*

Mark Cunningham, *Body Language*

Danielle Dutton, *Attempts at a Life*

Sarah Goldstein, *Fables*

Johannes Göransson, *Entrance to a colonial pageant in which we all begin to intricate*

Johannes Göransson, *Haute Surveillance*

Noah Eli Gordon & Joshua Marie Wilkinson, *Figures for a Darkroom Voice*

Dana Green, *Sometimes the Air in the Room Goes Missing*

Gordon Massman, *The Essential Numbers 1991 - 2008*

Joyelle McSweeney, *Nylund, The Sarcographer*

Kim Parko, *The Grotesque Child*

Joanna Ruocco, *Man's Companions*

Kim Gek Lin Short, *The Bugging Watch & Other Exhibits*

Kim Gek Lin Short, *China Cowboy*

Shelly Taylor, *Black-Eyed Heifer*

Max Winter, *The Pictures*

David Wolach, *Hospitalogy*

Andrew Zornoza, *Where I Stay*

CHAPBOOKS

Sandy Florian, *32 Pedals and 47 Stops*
James Haug, *Scratch*
Claire Hero, *Dollyland*
Paula Koneazny, *Installation*
Paul McCormick, *The Exotic Moods of Les Baxter*
Teresa K. Miller, *Forever No Lo*
Jeanne Morel, *That Crossing Is Not Automatic*
Andrew Michael Roberts, *Give Up*
Brandon Shimoda, *The Inland Sea*
Chad Sweeney, *A Mirror to Shatter the Hammer*
Emily Toder, *Brushes With*

G.C. Waldrep, *One Way No Exit*

&

Tarpaulin Sky Literary Journal
in print and online

tarpaulinsky.com